that we should LOVE on...

1 John 3:11 NKJV

Godly Love is or does the following...

Abundant ~ Amazing ~ Appreciative ~ Aware ~ Bears all things ~ Beautiful
Believes all things ~ Cares ~ Comforts ~ Committs ~ Compassionate ~ Content
Cooperative ~ Courteous ~ Dependable ~ Defends ~ Empathetic ~ Encourages
Endures ~ Extravagant ~ Fair ~ Faithful ~ Free ~ Friendly ~ Forgives ~ Fulfills
Generous ~ Gentle ~ Gives ~ Good ~ Gracious ~ Helpful ~ Hospitable ~ Inspires ~ Joyful
Kind ~ Honors ~ Hopeful ~ Listens ~ Magnificent ~ Obeys ~ Optimistic ~ Passionate
Patient ~ Plans ~ Protects ~ Prayerful ~ Reasonable ~ Repents ~ Respects ~ Sacrifices
Satisfies ~ Sensitive ~ Serves ~ Shares ~ Sincere ~ Strong ~ Supportive ~ Sweet ~ Teaches
Tender ~ Thankful ~ Thoughtful ~ Tolerant ~ Truthful ~ Trusts ~ Trustworthy
Understands ~ Unselfish ~ Values ~ Wonderful ~ Zealous

fear in love;
but perfect love
casts out fear,
because fear involves torment. But he who fears has not been made perfect in love.

1 John 4:18 NKJV

This is not to say that if you are experiencing fear
that you should feel condemned.
When we are in fear the most is when we are trusting God the least.
When we really know God's all-encompassing love for us, fear won't get the best of us.
We should all be striving
to grasp that LOVE!

God Is Real

by Beverly Rosas

Photos by Beverly Rosas, Milton Rosas and Elise Tang

This book is dedicated to my husband
Milton, who supports me in everything I do.

I know God is real.

Pacific Ocean

St. Thomas

Yosemite National Park

Kauai

Hulbert, Oklahoma

Kauai

The world He designed is a
magnificent and thrilling place to live!

When I awake to the clean, pale light each morning, I remember that God created the day and the night on the first day.

Florida

Each stroll on the beach reminds me of the second day, when God made the cerulean sky and sapphire ocean.

Hawaii

Hibiscus

Crepe Myrtle

California Poppy

Rose

Verbena

Bougainvillea

I delight in delicate flowers with
pastel, vivid and striking colors,

majestic,

General Grant Tree
Kings Canyon National Park

towering
trees,

General Sherman Tree
Sequoia National Park

soft blankets of grass,

delicious fruits,

Oranges

Grapes

and countless other plants that
God created on the third day.

Angel Oak, South Carolina

ColorBlaze Velveteen

Succulent

Spanish Moss on Oak tree
South Carolina

The bright, buttery glow of the sun

Sunset in Kauai

Full Moon

Waxing
Crescent

and the cool silvery light from the moon and stars
are proof of God's fourth day of work.

Butterfly fish, Clownfish, Yellow Tang, Blue Tang. Monterey Bay Aquarium

It is enchanting to see the vibrant, colorful fish,

Crab
Fanning Island

Humpback Whale
Avila Beach, California

Jellyfish, Monterey Bay Aquarium

mysterious sea
creatures,

Owl, Fresno Chaffee Zoo

Emu, Fresno Chaffee Zoo

Golden Eagle, Fresno Chaffee Zoo

Peacock, Kauai

Flamingos, Fresno Chaffee Zoo

Gull, St. Thomas

and brilliant, majestic birds that
God created on the fifth day.

Anteater, Fresno Chaffee Zoo

The animals of the world are comical,

exotic,

Panda, San Diego Zoo

Galapagos Tortoise,
Fresno Chaffee Zoo

Giraffes, Disney World Animal Kingdom

Snake, Fresno Chaffee Zoo

Gorilla, Disney World Animal Kingdom

Rhinoceros, Fresno Chaffee Zoo

terrifying,

and adorable.

God designed humans to be intelligent, emotional and imaginative like Him. All this on the sixth day of creation.

Hawaii

Sedona, Arizona

Fanning Island

Kauai

After considering the beauty, detail and design of this amazing world we live in, I know that God is real!

Made in the USA
Middletown, DE
22 April 2024

53298562R00015